STUDYING MADE EASY

This Craml0l notebook is designed to make studying easier and increase your comprehension of the textbook material. Instead of starting with a blank notebook and trying to write down everything discussed in class lectures, you can use this Craml0l textbook notebook and annotate your notes along with the lecture.

Our goal is to give you the best tools for success.

For a supreme understanding of the course, pair your notebook with our online tools. Should you decide you prefer Craml0l.com as your study tool,

we'd like to offer you a trade...

Our Trade In program is a simple way for us to keep our promise and provide you the best studying tools, regardless of where you purchased your Craml0l textbook notebook. As long as your notebook is in *Like New Condition**, you can send it back to us and we will immediately give you a Craml0l.com account free for 120 days!

Let The *Trade In* Begin!

THREE SIMPLE STEPS TO TRADE:

1. Go to www.cram101.com/tradein and fill out the packing slip information.

2. Submit and print the packing slip and mail it in with your Craml0l textbook notebook.

3. Activate your account after you receive your email confirmation.

* Books must be returned in *Like New Condition*, meaning there is no damage to the book including, but not limited to; ripped or torn pages, markings or writing on pages, or folded / creased pages. Upon receiving the book, Craml0l will inspect it and reserves the right to terminate your free Craml0l.com account and return your textbook notebook at the owners expense.

Learning System

Cram101 Textbook Outlines is a learning system. The notes in this book are the highlights of your textbook, you will never have to highlight a book again.

How to use this book. Take this book to class, it is your notebook for the lecture. The notes and highlights on the left hand side of the pages follow the outline and order of the textbook. All you have to do is follow along while your instructor presents the lecture. Circle the items emphasized in class and add other important information on the right side. With Cram101 Textbook Outlines you'll spend less time writing and more time listening. Learning becomes more efficient.

Cram101.com Online

Increase your studying efficiency by using Cram101.com's practice tests and online reference material. It is the perfect complement to Cram101 Textbook Outlines. Use self-teaching matching tests or simulate in-class testing with comprehensive multiple choice tests, or simply use Cram's true and false tests for quick review. Cram101.com even allows you to enter your in-class notes for an integrated studying format combining the textbook notes with your class notes.

Visit **www.Cram101.com**, click Sign Up at the top of the screen, and enter **DK73DW9618** in the promo code box on the registration screen. Your access to www.Cram101.com is discounted by 50% because you have purchased this book. Sign up and stop highlighting textbooks forever.

Cram101 Textbook Outlines to accompany:

Family Therapy Basics

Mark Worden, 3rd Edition

A Content Technologies Inc. publication (c) 2012.

Family Therapy Basics
Mark Worden, 3rd

CONTENTS

Chapter 1. The Movement to Systems and Social Construction

Engagement	An engagement is a promise to marry, and also the period of time between proposal and marriage - which may be lengthy or trivial. During this period, a couple is said to be affianced, betrothed, engaged to be married, or simply engaged. Future brides and grooms are often referred to as fiancées or fiancés respectively .
Epistemology	Epistemology is the branch of philosophy concerned with the nature and scope (limitations) of knowledge. It addresses the questions: • What is knowledge? • How is knowledge acquired? • How do we know what we know? In physics, the concept of epistemology is vital in the modern interpretation of quantum mechanics, and is used by many authors to analyse the works of dominant physicists such as Werner Heisenberg, Max Born and Wolfgang Pauli. Much of the debate in this field has focused on analyzing the nature of knowledge and how it relates to connected notions such as truth, belief, and justification.
Therapeutic alliance	The therapeutic alliance refers to the relationship between a healthcare professional and a client (or patient). It is the means by which the professional hopes to engage with, and affect change in a client. While much early work on this subject was generated from a psychodynamic perspective, researchers from other orientations have since investigated this area. It has been found to predict treatment adherence (compliance) and concordance and outcome across a range of client/patient diagnoses and treatment settings. Research on the statistical power of the therapeutic relationship now reflects more than 1,000 findings.
Salvador Minuchin	Salvador Minuchin is a family therapist born and raised in San Salvador, Entre Ríos, Argentina. He developed Structural Family Therapy, which addresses problems within a family by charting the relationships between family members, or between subsets of family. These charts represent power dynamics as well as the boundaries between different subsystems.

Chapter 1. The Movement to Systems and Social Construction

Homeostasis	Homeostasis is the property of a system, either open or closed, that regulates its internal environment and tends to maintain a stable, constant condition. Typically used to refer to a living organism, the concept came from that of milieu interieur that was created by Claude Bernard and published in 1865. Multiple dynamic equilibrium adjustment and regulation mechanisms make homeostasis possible.
Ontogeny	Ontogeny describes the origin and the development of an organism from the fertilized egg to its mature form. In more general terms, ontogeny is defined as the history of structural change in a unity, which can be a cell, an organism, or a society of organisms, without the loss of the organization which allows that unity to exist. More recently, the term ontogeny has been used in cell biology to describe the development of various cell types within an organism.
David Reiss	David Reiss is a Social Psychologist and Researcher. He currently is Vivian Gill Distinguished Research Professor at the George Washington University Medical Center, where he has also been Director of the Center for Family Research. His most notable contribution to the field came in 1981, when he published his monumental book, The Family's Construction of Reality.
Triangulation	Triangulation is most commonly used to express a situation in which one family member will not communicate directly with another family member, but will communicate with a third family member, which can lead to the third family member becoming part of the triangle. The concept originated in the study of dysfunctional family systems, but can describe behaviors in other systems as well, including work. Triangulation can also be used as a label for a form of "splitting" in which one person plays the third family member against one that he or she is upset about.
Family	In human context, a family is a group of people affiliated by consanguinity, affinity, or co-residence. In most societies it is the principal institution for the socialization of children. Extended from the human "family unit" by affinity, economy, culture, tradition, honor, and friendship are concepts of family that are metaphorical, or that grow increasingly inclusive extending to nationhood and humanism.

Chapter 1. The Movement to Systems and Social Construction

Causality	Causality is the relationship between an event (the cause) and a second event (the effect), where the second event is understood as a consequence of the first.
	Though the causes and effects are typically related to changes or events, candidates include objects, processes, properties, variables, facts, and states of affairs; characterizing the causal relationship can be the subject of much debate.
	The philosophical treatment of causality extends over millennia.
Communication	Communication is a process whereby meaning is defined and shared between living organisms. Communication requires a sender, a message, and an intended recipient, although the receiver need not be present or aware of the sender's intent to communicate at the time of communication; thus communication can occur across vast distances in time and space. Communication requires that the communicating parties share an area of communicative commonality.
Context	Context is a notion used in the language sciences (linguistics, sociolinguistics, discourse analysis, pragmatics, semiotics, etc). in two different ways, namely as • verbal context • social context Verbal context Verbal context refers to surrounding text or talk of an expression (word, sentence, conversational turn, speech act, etc).. The idea is that verbal context influences the way we understand the expression.
Constructionism	Constructionist learning is inspired by the constructivist theory that individual learners construct mental models to understand the world around them. However, constructionism holds that learning can happen most effectively when people are also active in making tangible objects in the real world. In this sense, constructionism is connected with experiential learning and builds on some of the ideas of Jean Piaget.

Chapter 1. The Movement to Systems and Social Construction

Perspective	Perspective, in context of vision and visual perception, is the way in which objects appear to the eye based on their spatial attributes; or their dimensions and the position of the eye relative to the objects. There are two main meanings of the term: linear perspective and aerial perspective. Linear perspective As objects become more distant they appear smaller because their visual angle decreases.
Social constructionism	Social constructionism and social constructivism are sociological theories of knowledge that consider how social phenomena or objects of consciousness develop in social contexts. Within constructionist thought, a social construction (social construct) is a concept or practice that is the construct (or artifact) of a particular group. When we say that something is socially constructed, we are focusing on its dependence on contingent variables of our social selves rather than any inherent quality that it possesses in itself.
Theory	Originally the word theory is a technical term from Ancient Greek. It is derived from theoria, θεωρ? α, meaning "a looking at, viewing, beholding", and refers to contemplation or speculation, as opposed to action. Theory is especially often contrasted to "practice" a concept that in its original Aristotelian context referred to actions done for their own sake, but can also refer to "technical" actions instrumental to some other aim, such as the making of tools or houses.
Therapy	Therapy is the attempted remediation of a health problem, usually following a diagnosis. In the medical field, it is synonymous with the word "treatment". Among psychologists, the term may refer specifically to psychotherapy or "talk therapy".
Cybernetics	Cybernetics is the interdisciplinary study of the structure of regulatory systems. Cybernetics is closely related to control theory and systems theory. Both in its origins and in its evolution in the second-half of the 20th century, cybernetics is equally applicable to physical and social (that is, language-based) systems.

Chapter 1. The Movement to Systems and Social Construction

Adolescence	Adolescence is a transitional stage of physical and mental human development generally occurring between puberty and legal adulthood (age of majority), but largely characterized as beginning and ending with the teenage stage. According to Erik Erikson's stages of human development, for example, a young adult is generally a person between the ages of 20 and 40, whereas an adolescent is a person between the ages of 13 and 19. Historically, puberty has been heavily associated with teenagers and the onset of adolescent development. However, the start of puberty has had somewhat of an increase in preadolescence and adolescence has had an occasional extension beyond the teenage years (typically males) compared to previous generations.
Diagnostic and Statistical Manual of Mental Disorders	The Diagnostic and Statistical Manual of Mental Disorders is published by the American Psychiatric Association and provides a common language and standard criteria for the classification of mental disorders. It is used in the United States and in varying degrees around the world, by clinicians, researchers, psychiatric drug regulation agencies, health insurance companies, pharmaceutical companies, and policy makers. The DSM has attracted controversy and criticism as well as praise.
Mental Disorder	A mental disorder is a psychological or behavioral pattern generally associated with subjective distress or disability that occurs in an individual, and which is not a part of normal development or culture. The recognition and understanding of mental health conditions has changed over time and across cultures, and there are still variations in the definition, assessment, and classification of mental disorders, although standard guideline criteria are widely accepted. A few mental disorders are diagnosed based on the harm to others, regardless of the subject's perception of distress.
Diagnosis	As a subfield in artificial intelligence, Diagnosis is concerned with the development of algorithms and techniques that are able to determine whether the behaviour of a system is correct. If the system is not functioning correctly, the algorithm should be able to determine, as accurately as possible, which part of the system is failing, and which kind of fault it is facing. The computation is based on observations, which provide information on the current behaviour.

Chapter 2. The First Interview: Initiating Assessment and Engagement

Death	Death is the termination of the biological functions that sustain a living organism. The word refers both to the particular processes of life's cessation as well as to the condition or state of a formerly living body. Phenomena which commonly bring about death include predation, malnutrition, accidents resulting in terminal injury, and disease.
Diagnosis	As a subfield in artificial intelligence, Diagnosis is concerned with the development of algorithms and techniques that are able to determine whether the behaviour of a system is correct. If the system is not functioning correctly, the algorithm should be able to determine, as accurately as possible, which part of the system is failing, and which kind of fault it is facing. The computation is based on observations, which provide information on the current behaviour.
Interview	An interview is a conversation between two people (the interviewer and the interviewee) where questions are asked by the interviewer to obtain information from the interviewee.
	Types of interviews
	Others
	Publications

Several publications give prominence to interviews, including:

- Interviews with novelists conducted since 1950 by The Paris Review
- Interviews with celebrities conducted by Interview magazine, co-founded by Andy Warhol in 1969
- The Rolling Stone Interview, featured in Rolling Stone magazine

Famous interviews

- 1957-1960: The Mike Wallace Interview - 30-minute television interviews conducted by Mike Wallace
- 1968: Interviews with Phil Ochs - an interview of folk singer Phil Ochs conducted by Broadside Magazine
- 1974: Michael Parkinson/Muhammad Ali - television interview of Ali in his prime
- 1977: Frost/Nixon interviews - 1977 television interviews by British journalist David Frost of former United States President Richard Nixon
- early 1980s: Soviet Interview Project - conducted with Soviet emigrants to the United States
- 1992: Fellini: I'm a Born Liar - Federico Fellini's last filmed interviews conducted in 1992 for a 2002 feature documentary
- 1992: Nevermind It's an Interview - interviews with the band Nirvana recorded in 1992 on the night they appeared on Saturday Night Live
- 1993: Michael Jackson talks to Oprah Winfrey. This became the fourth most watched event in American television history as well as the most watched interview ever, with an audience of one hundred million.
- 1993: Birthday Cake Interview - an interview of Dr. John Hewson that contributed to the defeat of his party in the 1993 Australian federal election
- 2002-3: Living with Michael Jackson - a 2002-3 interview with Michael Jackson, later turned into a documentary
- 2003: February 2003 Saddam Hussein interview - Dan Rather interviewing Saddam Hussein days before the 2003 invasion of Iraq
- 2008: Sarah Palin interviews with Katie Couric? - Katie Couric interviewing Sarah Palin

Chapter 2. The First Interview: Initiating Assessment and Engagement

Capacity	The capacity of both natural and legal persons determines whether they may make binding amendments to their rights, duties and obligations, such as getting married or merging, entering into contracts, making gifts, or writing a valid will. Capacity is an aspect of status and both are defined by a person's personal law: • for natural persons, the law of domicile or lex domicilii in common law jurisdictions, and either the law of nationality or lex patriae, or of habitual residence in civil law states; • for legal persons, the law of the place of incorporation, the lex incorporationis for companies while other forms of business entity derive their capacity either from the law of the place in which they were formed or the laws of the states in which they establish a presence for trading purposes depending on the nature of the entity and the transactions entered into. When the law limits or bars a person from engaging in specified activities, any agreements or contracts to do so are either voidable or void for incapacity. Sometimes such legal incapacity is referred to as incompetence.
Family	In human context, a family is a group of people affiliated by consanguinity, affinity, or co-residence. In most societies it is the principal institution for the socialization of children. Extended from the human "family unit" by affinity, economy, culture, tradition, honor, and friendship are concepts of family that are metaphorical, or that grow increasingly inclusive extending to nationhood and humanism.
Scapegoating	Scapegoating is the practice of singling out any party for unmerited negative treatment or blame. A scapegoat may be a child, employee, peer, ethnic or religious group, or country. A whipping boy or "fall guy" is a form of scapegoat.
Triangulation	Triangulation is most commonly used to express a situation in which one family member will not communicate directly with another family member, but will communicate with a third family member, which can lead to the third family member becoming part of the triangle. The concept originated in the study of dysfunctional family systems, but can describe behaviors in other systems as well, including work.

Chapter 2. The First Interview: Initiating Assessment and Engagement

	Triangulation can also be used as a label for a form of "splitting" in which one person plays the third family member against one that he or she is upset about.
Salvador Minuchin	Salvador Minuchin is a family therapist born and raised in San Salvador, Entre Ríos, Argentina. He developed Structural Family Therapy, which addresses problems within a family by charting the relationships between family members, or between subsets of family. These charts represent power dynamics as well as the boundaries between different subsystems.
Concept	A concept is a cognitive unit of meaning--an abstract idea or a mental symbol sometimes defined as a "unit of knowledge," built from other units which act as a concept's characteristics. A concept is typically associated with a corresponding representation in a language or symbology such as a single meaning of a term. There are prevailing theories in contemporary philosophy which attempt to explain the nature of concepts.
Robert-Jay Green	Robert-Jay Green, Ph.D is the Founder and Executive Director of the Rockway Institute, and is the Distinguished Professor in the Clinical Psychology PhD Program at the California School of Professional Psychology at Alliant International University. About Green's main areas of research over the last 30 years have included gay and lesbian couples and families; male gender role socialization; the measurement of couple and family relationship processes; multicultural issues in family functioning; the impact of family relations on children's academic achievement; and couple and family therapy.

Green previously served as Executive Director and President of the board of the non-profit Alternative Family Institute in San Francisco (the nation's first counseling center exclusively devoted to LGBT couple and family issues) and as Founder and Co-Director of Redwood Center Psychology Associates in Berkeley (one of the San Francisco Bay Area's leading couple and family therapy training centers).

Communication	Communication is a process whereby meaning is defined and shared between living organisms. Communication requires a sender, a message, and an intended recipient, although the receiver need not be present or aware of the sender's intent to communicate at the time of communication; thus communication can occur across vast distances in time and space. Communication requires that the communicating parties share an area of communicative commonality.
Phon	The phon was proposed in DIN 45631 and ISO 532 B as a unit of perceived loudness level L_N for pure tones by S. S. Stevens. The purpose of the phon scale is to compensate for the effect of frequency on the perceived loudness of tones. By definition, 1 phon is equal to 1 dBSPL at a frequency of 1 kHz.

21

Chapter 3. Engagement: Establishing Therapeutic Boundaries

Rating Scale	A rating scale is a set of categorize designed to elicit information about a quantitative or a qualitative attribute. In the social sciences, common examples are the Likert scale and 1-10 rating scales in which a person selects the number which is considered to reflect the perceived quality of a product. A rating scale is an instrument that requires the rater to assign the rated object that have numerals assigned to them.
Family	In human context, a family is a group of people affiliated by consanguinity, affinity, or co-residence. In most societies it is the principal institution for the socialization of children. Extended from the human "family unit" by affinity, economy, culture, tradition, honor, and friendship are concepts of family that are metaphorical, or that grow increasingly inclusive extending to nationhood and humanism.
David Reiss	David Reiss is a Social Psychologist and Researcher. He currently is Vivian Gill Distinguished Research Professor at the George Washington University Medical Center, where he has also been Director of the Center for Family Research. His most notable contribution to the field came in 1981, when he published his monumental book, The Family's Construction of Reality.
Constructionism	Constructionist learning is inspired by the constructivist theory that individual learners construct mental models to understand the world around them. However, constructionism holds that learning can happen most effectively when people are also active in making tangible objects in the real world. In this sense, constructionism is connected with experiential learning and builds on some of the ideas of Jean Piaget.
Social constructionism	Social constructionism and social constructivism are sociological theories of knowledge that consider how social phenomena or objects of consciousness develop in social contexts. Within constructionist thought, a social construction (social construct) is a concept or practice that is the construct (or artifact) of a particular group. When we say that something is socially constructed, we are focusing on its dependence on contingent variables of our social selves rather than any inherent quality that it possesses in itself.

Chapter 3. Engagement: Establishing Therapeutic Boundaries

Communication	Communication is a process whereby meaning is defined and shared between living organisms. Communication requires a sender, a message, and an intended recipient, although the receiver need not be present or aware of the sender's intent to communicate at the time of communication; thus communication can occur across vast distances in time and space. Communication requires that the communicating parties share an area of communicative commonality.
Model	Art models are models who pose for photographers, painters, sculptors, and other artists as part of their work of art. Art models are often paid, sometimes even professional, human subjects, who aid in creating a portrait or other work of art including such figure wholly or partially. Models are frequently used for training art students, but are also employed by accomplished artists.
Paradigm	In the behavioural sciences, e.g. Psychology, Biology, Neurosciences, an experimental paradigm is an experimental setup (i.e. a way to conduct a certain type of experiment) that is defined by certain fine-tuned standards and often has a theoretical background. A paradigm in this technical sense, however, is not a way of thinking as it is in the epistemological meaning.
Genogram	A genogram is a pictorial display of a person's family relationships and medical history. It goes beyond a traditional family tree by allowing the user to visualize hereditary patterns and psychological factors that punctuate relationships. It can be used to identify repetitive patterns of behavior and to recognize hereditary tendencies.
Theory	Originally the word theory is a technical term from Ancient Greek. It is derived from theoria, θεωρ?α, meaning "a looking at, viewing, beholding", and refers to contemplation or speculation, as opposed to action. Theory is especially often contrasted to "practice" a concept that in its original Aristotelian context referred to actions done for their own sake, but can also refer to "technical" actions instrumental to some other aim, such as the making of tools or houses.
Triangulation	Triangulation is most commonly used to express a situation in which one family member will not communicate directly with another family member, but will communicate with a third family member, which can lead to the third family member becoming part of the triangle. The concept originated in the study of dysfunctional family systems, but can describe behaviors in other systems as well, including work.

Triangulation can also be used as a label for a form of "splitting" in which one person plays the third family member against one that he or she is upset about.

| Robert-Jay Green | Robert-Jay Green, Ph.D is the Founder and Executive Director of the Rockway Institute, and is the Distinguished Professor in the Clinical Psychology PhD Program at the California School of Professional Psychology at Alliant International University. |

About

Green's main areas of research over the last 30 years have included gay and lesbian couples and families; male gender role socialization; the measurement of couple and family relationship processes; multicultural issues in family functioning; the impact of family relations on children's academic achievement; and couple and family therapy.

Green previously served as Executive Director and President of the board of the non-profit Alternative Family Institute in San Francisco (the nation's first counseling center exclusively devoted to LGBT couple and family issues) and as Founder and Co-Director of Redwood Center Psychology Associates in Berkeley (one of the San Francisco Bay Area's leading couple and family therapy training centers).

| Bias | In statistics, the term bias refers to several different concepts: |

- Selection bias, where individuals or groups are more likely to take part in a research project than others, resulting in biased samples. This can also be termed Berksonian bias.
  - Spectrum bias arises from evaluating diagnostic tests on biased patient samples, leading to an overestimate of the sensitivity and specificity of the test.
- The bias of an estimator is the difference between an estimator's expectation and the true value of the parameter being estimated.

Chapter 3. Engagement: Establishing Therapeutic Boundaries

Therapeutic alliance	The therapeutic alliance refers to the relationship between a healthcare professional and a client (or patient). It is the means by which the professional hopes to engage with, and affect change in a client. While much early work on this subject was generated from a psychodynamic perspective, researchers from other orientations have since investigated this area. It has been found to predict treatment adherence (compliance) and concordance and outcome across a range of client/patient diagnoses and treatment settings. Research on the statistical power of the therapeutic relationship now reflects more than 1,000 findings.
Scapegoating	Scapegoating is the practice of singling out any party for unmerited negative treatment or blame. A scapegoat may be a child, employee, peer, ethnic or religious group, or country. A whipping boy or "fall guy" is a form of scapegoat.
Concept	A concept is a cognitive unit of meaning--an abstract idea or a mental symbol sometimes defined as a "unit of knowledge," built from other units which act as a concept's characteristics. A concept is typically associated with a corresponding representation in a language or symbology such as a single meaning of a term. There are prevailing theories in contemporary philosophy which attempt to explain the nature of concepts.
Narrative	A narrative is a story that is created in a constructive format (as a work of speech, writing, song, film, television, video games, in photography or theatre) that describes a sequence of fictional or non-fictional events. Ultimately its origin is found in the Proto-Indo-European root gno-, "to know". The word "story" may be used as a synonym of "narrative", but can also be used to refer to the sequence of events described in a narrative.
Therapy	Therapy is the attempted remediation of a health problem, usually following a diagnosis. In the medical field, it is synonymous with the word "treatment". Among psychologists, the term may refer specifically to psychotherapy or "talk therapy".

Chapter 3. Engagement: Establishing Therapeutic Boundaries

Death	Death is the termination of the biological functions that sustain a living organism. The word refers both to the particular processes of life's cessation as well as to the condition or state of a formerly living body. Phenomena which commonly bring about death include predation, malnutrition, accidents resulting in terminal injury, and disease.
Interview	An interview is a conversation between two people (the interviewer and the interviewee) where questions are asked by the interviewer to obtain information from the interviewee.

Types of interviews

Others

Publications |

Several publications give prominence to interviews, including:

- Interviews with novelists conducted since 1950 by The Paris Review
- Interviews with celebrities conducted by Interview magazine, co-founded by Andy Warhol in 1969
- The Rolling Stone Interview, featured in Rolling Stone magazine

Famous interviews

- 1957-1960: The Mike Wallace Interview - 30-minute television interviews conducted by Mike Wallace
- 1968: Interviews with Phil Ochs - an interview of folk singer Phil Ochs conducted by Broadside Magazine
- 1974: Michael Parkinson/Muhammad Ali - television interview of Ali in his prime
- 1977: Frost/Nixon interviews - 1977 television interviews by British journalist David Frost of former United States President Richard Nixon
- early 1980s: Soviet Interview Project - conducted with Soviet emigrants to the United States
- 1992: Fellini: I'm a Born Liar - Federico Fellini's last filmed interviews conducted in 1992 for a 2002 feature documentary
- 1992: Nevermind It's an Interview - interviews with the band Nirvana recorded in 1992 on the night they appeared on Saturday Night Live
- 1993: Michael Jackson talks to Oprah Winfrey. This became the fourth most watched event in American television history as well as the most watched interview ever, with an audience of one hundred million.
- 1993: Birthday Cake Interview - an interview of Dr. John Hewson that contributed to the defeat of his party in the 1993 Australian federal election
- 2002-3: Living with Michael Jackson - a 2002-3 interview with Michael Jackson, later turned into a documentary
- 2003: February 2003 Saddam Hussein interview - Dan Rather interviewing Saddam Hussein days before the 2003 invasion of Iraq
- 2008: Sarah Palin interviews with Katie Couric? - Katie Couric interviewing Sarah Palin

.

| Self-disclosure | Self-disclosure is both the conscious and unconscious act of revealing more about oneself to others. This may include, but is not limited to, thoughts, feelings, aspirations, goals, failures, successes, fears, dreams as well as one's likes, dislikes, and favorites. |

Typically, a self-disclosure happens when we initially meet someone and continues as we build and develop our relationships with people. As we get to know each other, we disclose information about ourselves. If one person is not willing to "self-disclose" then the other person may stop disclosing information about themselves as well.

Chapter 4. Assessment: Diagnosis and Systems Models

Death	Death is the termination of the biological functions that sustain a living organism. The word refers both to the particular processes of life's cessation as well as to the condition or state of a formerly living body. Phenomena which commonly bring about death include predation, malnutrition, accidents resulting in terminal injury, and disease.
Diagnostic and Statistical Manual of Mental Disorders	The Diagnostic and Statistical Manual of Mental Disorders is published by the American Psychiatric Association and provides a common language and standard criteria for the classification of mental disorders. It is used in the United States and in varying degrees around the world, by clinicians, researchers, psychiatric drug regulation agencies, health insurance companies, pharmaceutical companies, and policy makers. The DSM has attracted controversy and criticism as well as praise.
Family	In human context, a family is a group of people affiliated by consanguinity, affinity, or co-residence. In most societies it is the principal institution for the socialization of children. Extended from the human "family unit" by affinity, economy, culture, tradition, honor, and friendship are concepts of family that are metaphorical, or that grow increasingly inclusive extending to nationhood and humanism.
Mental Disorder	A mental disorder is a psychological or behavioral pattern generally associated with subjective distress or disability that occurs in an individual, and which is not a part of normal development or culture. The recognition and understanding of mental health conditions has changed over time and across cultures, and there are still variations in the definition, assessment, and classification of mental disorders, although standard guideline criteria are widely accepted. A few mental disorders are diagnosed based on the harm to others, regardless of the subject's perception of distress.
Model	Art models are models who pose for photographers, painters, sculptors, and other artists as part of their work of art. Art models are often paid, sometimes even professional, human subjects, who aid in creating a portrait or other work of art including such figure wholly or partially. Models are frequently used for training art students, but are also employed by accomplished artists.

CRAM101

Chapter 4. Assessment: Diagnosis and Systems Models

Diagnosis	As a subfield in artificial intelligence, Diagnosis is concerned with the development of algorithms and techniques that are able to determine whether the behaviour of a system is correct. If the system is not functioning correctly, the algorithm should be able to determine, as accurately as possible, which part of the system is failing, and which kind of fault it is facing. The computation is based on observations, which provide information on the current behaviour.
David Reiss	David Reiss is a Social Psychologist and Researcher. He currently is Vivian Gill Distinguished Research Professor at the George Washington University Medical Center, where he has also been Director of the Center for Family Research. His most notable contribution to the field came in 1981, when he published his monumental book, The Family's Construction of Reality.
Schizophrenia	Schizophrenia is a mental disorder characterized by a disintegration of thought processes and of emotional responsiveness. It most commonly manifests as auditory hallucinations, paranoid or bizarre delusions, or disorganized speech and thinking, and it is accompanied by significant social or occupational dysfunction. The onset of symptoms typically occurs in young adulthood, with a global lifetime prevalence of about 0.3-0.7%.
Triangulation	Triangulation is most commonly used to express a situation in which one family member will not communicate directly with another family member, but will communicate with a third family member, which can lead to the third family member becoming part of the triangle. The concept originated in the study of dysfunctional family systems, but can describe behaviors in other systems as well, including work. Triangulation can also be used as a label for a form of "splitting" in which one person plays the third family member against one that he or she is upset about.
Beavers	Beavers in Scouting is one name for the youngest section of Scouting with members (most commonly boys) younger than Cub Scouts and sometimes going to as young as five years of age. Other names are used in some countries. The programme is based on the concept of co-operating and sharing.
Rating Scale	A rating scale is a set of categorize designed to elicit information about a quantitative or a qualitative attribute. In the social sciences, common examples are the Likert scale and 1-10 rating scales in which a person selects the number which is considered to reflect the perceived quality of a product.

Chapter 4. Assessment: Diagnosis and Systems Models

A rating scale is an instrument that requires the rater to assign the rated object that have numerals assigned to them.

Flexibility

Flexibility is a personality trait -- the extent to which a person can cope with changes in circumstances and think about problems and tasks in novel, creative ways.

Causality

Causality is the relationship between an event (the cause) and a second event (the effect), where the second event is understood as a consequence of the first.

Though the causes and effects are typically related to changes or events, candidates include objects, processes, properties, variables, facts, and states of affairs; characterizing the causal relationship can be the subject of much debate.

The philosophical treatment of causality extends over millennia.

Competence

In American law, competence concerns the mental capacity of an individual to participate in legal proceedings. Defendants that do not possess sufficient "competence" are usually excluded from criminal prosecution, while witnesses found not to possess requisite competence cannot testify. The English equivalent is fitness to plead.

Mid-range

In statistics, the mid-range is the arithmetic mean of the maximum and minimum values in a data set, or:

$$M = \frac{\max x + \min x}{2}.$$

As such it is a measure of central tendency.

Chapter 4. Assessment: Diagnosis and Systems Models

	The midrange is highly sensitive to outliers and ignores all but two data points. It is therefore a very non-robust statistic (having a breakdown point of 0, meaning that a single observation can change it arbitrarily), and it is rarely used in statistical analysis.
Therapeutic alliance	The therapeutic alliance refers to the relationship between a healthcare professional and a client (or patient). It is the means by which the professional hopes to engage with, and affect change in a client.

While much early work on this subject was generated from a psychodynamic perspective, researchers from other orientations have since investigated this area. It has been found to predict treatment adherence (compliance) and concordance and outcome across a range of client/patient diagnoses and treatment settings. Research on the statistical power of the therapeutic relationship now reflects more than 1,000 findings. |
| Therapy | Therapy is the attempted remediation of a health problem, usually following a diagnosis. In the medical field, it is synonymous with the word "treatment". Among psychologists, the term may refer specifically to psychotherapy or "talk therapy". |
| Interview | An interview is a conversation between two people (the interviewer and the interviewee) where questions are asked by the interviewer to obtain information from the interviewee.

Types of interviews

Others

Publications |

Chapter 4. Assessment: Diagnosis and Systems Models

Several publications give prominence to interviews, including:

- Interviews with novelists conducted since 1950 by The Paris Review
- Interviews with celebrities conducted by Interview magazine, co-founded by Andy Warhol in 1969
- The Rolling Stone Interview, featured in Rolling Stone magazine

Famous interviews

- 1957-1960: The Mike Wallace Interview - 30-minute television interviews conducted by Mike Wallace
- 1968: Interviews with Phil Ochs - an interview of folk singer Phil Ochs conducted by Broadside Magazine
- 1974: Michael Parkinson/Muhammad Ali - television interview of Ali in his prime
- 1977: Frost/Nixon interviews - 1977 television interviews by British journalist David Frost of former United States President Richard Nixon
- early 1980s: Soviet Interview Project - conducted with Soviet emigrants to the United States
- 1992: Fellini: I'm a Born Liar - Federico Fellini's last filmed interviews conducted in 1992 for a 2002 feature documentary
- 1992: Nevermind It's an Interview - interviews with the band Nirvana recorded in 1992 on the night they appeared on Saturday Night Live
- 1993: Michael Jackson talks to Oprah Winfrey. This became the fourth most watched event in American television history as well as the most watched interview ever, with an audience of one hundred million.
- 1993: Birthday Cake Interview - an interview of Dr. John Hewson that contributed to the defeat of his party in the 1993 Australian federal election
- 2002-3: Living with Michael Jackson - a 2002-3 interview with Michael Jackson, later turned into a documentary
- 2003: February 2003 Saddam Hussein interview - Dan Rather interviewing Saddam Hussein days before the 2003 invasion of Iraq
- 2008: Sarah Palin interviews with Katie Couric? - Katie Couric interviewing Sarah Palin

.

Structured Interview	A structured interview is a quantitative research method commonly employed in survey research. The aim of this approach is to ensure that each interview is presented with exactly the same questions in the same order. This ensures that answers can be reliably aggregated and that comparisons can be made with confidence between sample subgroups or between different survey periods.

Chapter 4. Assessment: Diagnosis and Systems Models

Leadership	Leadership has been described as the "process of social influence in which one person can enlist the aid and support of others in the accomplishment of a common task". Definitions more inclusive of followers have also emerged. Alan Keith of Genentech states that, "Leadership is ultimately about creating a way for people to contribute to making something extraordinary happen." According to Ken "SKC" Ogbonnia, "effective leadership is the ability to successfully integrate and maximize available resources within the internal and external environment for the attainment of organizational or societal goals."
Communication	Communication is a process whereby meaning is defined and shared between living organisms. Communication requires a sender, a message, and an intended recipient, although the receiver need not be present or aware of the sender's intent to communicate at the time of communication; thus communication can occur across vast distances in time and space. Communication requires that the communicating parties share an area of communicative commonality.

Chapter 5. Assessment:The Process of Identifying Family Patterns

Beavers	Beavers in Scouting is one name for the youngest section of Scouting with members (most commonly boys) younger than Cub Scouts and sometimes going to as young as five years of age. Other names are used in some countries. The programme is based on the concept of co-operating and sharing.
Family	In human context, a family is a group of people affiliated by consanguinity, affinity, or co-residence. In most societies it is the principal institution for the socialization of children. Extended from the human "family unit" by affinity, economy, culture, tradition, honor, and friendship are concepts of family that are metaphorical, or that grow increasingly inclusive extending to nationhood and humanism.
Model	Art models are models who pose for photographers, painters, sculptors, and other artists as part of their work of art. Art models are often paid, sometimes even professional, human subjects, who aid in creating a portrait or other work of art including such figure wholly or partially. Models are frequently used for training art students, but are also employed by accomplished artists.
Genogram	A genogram is a pictorial display of a person's family relationships and medical history. It goes beyond a traditional family tree by allowing the user to visualize hereditary patterns and psychological factors that punctuate relationships. It can be used to identify repetitive patterns of behavior and to recognize hereditary tendencies.
Interview	An interview is a conversation between two people (the interviewer and the interviewee) where questions are asked by the interviewer to obtain information from the interviewee. Types of interviews Others Publications

Several publications give prominence to interviews, including:

- Interviews with novelists conducted since 1950 by The Paris Review
- Interviews with celebrities conducted by Interview magazine, co-founded by Andy Warhol in 1969
- The Rolling Stone Interview, featured in Rolling Stone magazine

Famous interviews

- 1957-1960: The Mike Wallace Interview - 30-minute television interviews conducted by Mike Wallace
- 1968: Interviews with Phil Ochs - an interview of folk singer Phil Ochs conducted by Broadside Magazine
- 1974: Michael Parkinson/Muhammad Ali - television interview of Ali in his prime
- 1977: Frost/Nixon interviews - 1977 television interviews by British journalist David Frost of former United States President Richard Nixon
- early 1980s: Soviet Interview Project - conducted with Soviet emigrants to the United States
- 1992: Fellini: I'm a Born Liar - Federico Fellini's last filmed interviews conducted in 1992 for a 2002 feature documentary
- 1992: Nevermind It's an Interview - interviews with the band Nirvana recorded in 1992 on the night they appeared on Saturday Night Live
- 1993: Michael Jackson talks to Oprah Winfrey. This became the fourth most watched event in American television history as well as the most watched interview ever, with an audience of one hundred million.
- 1993: Birthday Cake Interview - an interview of Dr. John Hewson that contributed to the defeat of his party in the 1993 Australian federal election
- 2002-3: Living with Michael Jackson - a 2002-3 interview with Michael Jackson, later turned into a documentary
- 2003: February 2003 Saddam Hussein interview - Dan Rather interviewing Saddam Hussein days before the 2003 invasion of Iraq
- 2008: Sarah Palin interviews with Katie Couric? - Katie Couric interviewing Sarah Palin

Cognition

Cognition is the scientific term for "the process of thought". Usage of the term varies in different disciplines; for example in psychology and cognitive science, it usually refers to an information processing view of an individual's psychological functions. Other interpretations of the meaning of cognition link it to the development of concepts; individual minds, groups, and organizations.

Chapter 5. Assessment:The Process of Identifying Family Patterns

Exploring	Exploring is a worksite-based program of Learning for Life, a subsidiary of the Boy Scouts of America, for young men and women who are 14 through 20 years old (15 through 21 in some areas). Exploring units, called "posts", usually have a focus on a single career field, such as police, fire/rescue, health, law, aviation, engineering, or the like, and may be sponsored by a government or business entity. Prior to the late 1990s, the Exploring program was the main BSA program for older youth and included posts with an emphasis on outdoor activities, which are now part of the Venturing program.
Prediction	A prediction is a statement about the way things will happen in the future, often but not always based on experience or knowledge. While there is much overlap between prediction and forecast, a prediction may be a statement that some outcome is expected, while a forecast may cover a range of possible outcomes. Although guaranteed information about the information is in many cases impossible, prediction is necessary to allow plans to be made about possible developments; Howard H. Stevenson writes that prediction in business "... is at least two things: Important and hard." Prediction is closely related to uncertainty.
Diagnosis	As a subfield in artificial intelligence, Diagnosis is concerned with the development of algorithms and techniques that are able to determine whether the behaviour of a system is correct. If the system is not functioning correctly, the algorithm should be able to determine, as accurately as possible, which part of the system is failing, and which kind of fault it is facing. The computation is based on observations, which provide information on the current behaviour.
Play	Play refers to a range of voluntary, intrinsically motivated activities that are normally associated with pleasure and enjoyment. Play is essentially an activity which a person enjoys alone, though it can involve others, who perceive the play from their perspective and may not be in the mood for play. Play is most commonly associated with child activities, and when engaged in by an adult they may be described as "childish" or "child at heart".

Chapter 5. Assessment: The Process of Identifying Family Patterns

Understanding	Understanding is a psychological process related to an abstract or physical object, such as a person, situation, or message whereby one is able to think about it and use concepts to deal adequately with that object. An understanding is the limit of a conceptualization. To understand something is to have conceptualized it to a given measure.
Bias	In statistics, the term bias refers to several different concepts: • Selection bias, where individuals or groups are more likely to take part in a research project than others, resulting in biased samples. This can also be termed Berksonian bias. ○ Spectrum bias arises from evaluating diagnostic tests on biased patient samples, leading to an overestimate of the sensitivity and specificity of the test. • The bias of an estimator is the difference between an estimator's expectation and the true value of the parameter being estimated.
Cultural bias	Cultural bias is the phenomenon of interpreting and judging phenomena by standards inherent to one's own culture. The phenomenon is sometimes considered a problem central to social and human sciences, such as economics, psychology, anthropology, and sociology. Some practitioners of the aforementioned fields have attempted to develop methods and theories to compensate for or eliminate cultural bias.
Family therapy	Family therapy, also referred to as couple and family therapy and family systems therapy, is a branch of psychotherapy that works with families and couples in intimate relationships to nurture change and development. It tends to view change in terms of the systems of interaction between family members. It emphasizes family relationships as an important factor in psychological health.
Resistance	"Resistance" as initially used by Sigmund Freud, referred to patients blocking memories from conscious memory. This was a key concept, since the primary treatment method of Freud's talk therapy required making these memories available to the patient's consciousness. "Resistance" expanded

	Later, Freud described five different forms of resistance.
Therapeutic alliance	The therapeutic alliance refers to the relationship between a healthcare professional and a client (or patient). It is the means by which the professional hopes to engage with, and affect change in a client. While much early work on this subject was generated from a psychodynamic perspective, researchers from other orientations have since investigated this area. It has been found to predict treatment adherence (compliance) and concordance and outcome across a range of client/patient diagnoses and treatment settings. Research on the statistical power of the therapeutic relationship now reflects more than 1,000 findings.
Stepfamily	A stepfamily, is a family in which one or both members of the couple have children from a previous relationship. The member of the couple to whom the child is not biologically related is the stepparent, specifically the stepmother or stepfather. The traditional and strictest definition of a "stepfamily" is a married couple where one or both members of the couple have pre-existing children who live with them.
Resilience	Resilience is the property of a material to absorb energy when it is deformed elastically and then, upon unloading to have this energy recovered. In other words, it is the maximum energy per unit volume that can be elastically stored. It is represented by the area under the curve in the elastic region in the stress-strain curve.
Intervention	An intervention is an orchestrated attempt by one, or often many, people (usually family and friends) to get someone to seek professional help with an addiction or some kind of traumatic event or crisis, or other serious problem. The term intervention is most often used when the traumatic event involves addiction to drugs or other items. Intervention can also refer to the act of using a technique within a therapy session.
Death	Death is the termination of the biological functions that sustain a living organism. The word refers both to the particular processes of life's cessation as well as to the condition or state of a formerly living body. Phenomena which commonly bring about death include predation, malnutrition, accidents resulting in terminal injury, and disease.

Chapter 5. Assessment: The Process of Identifying Family Patterns

Triangulation	Triangulation is most commonly used to express a situation in which one family member will not communicate directly with another family member, but will communicate with a third family member, which can lead to the third family member becoming part of the triangle. The concept originated in the study of dysfunctional family systems, but can describe behaviors in other systems as well, including work. Triangulation can also be used as a label for a form of "splitting" in which one person plays the third family member against one that he or she is upset about.

Chapter 6. Change and Resistance

Causality	Causality is the relationship between an event (the cause) and a second event (the effect), where the second event is understood as a consequence of the first. Though the causes and effects are typically related to changes or events, candidates include objects, processes, properties, variables, facts, and states of affairs; characterizing the causal relationship can be the subject of much debate. The philosophical treatment of causality extends over millennia.
Salvador Minuchin	Salvador Minuchin is a family therapist born and raised in San Salvador, Entre Ríos, Argentina. He developed Structural Family Therapy, which addresses problems within a family by charting the relationships between family members, or between subsets of family. These charts represent power dynamics as well as the boundaries between different subsystems.
Ontogeny	Ontogeny describes the origin and the development of an organism from the fertilized egg to its mature form. In more general terms, ontogeny is defined as the history of structural change in a unity, which can be a cell, an organism, or a society of organisms, without the loss of the organization which allows that unity to exist. More recently, the term ontogeny has been used in cell biology to describe the development of various cell types within an organism.
David Reiss	David Reiss is a Social Psychologist and Researcher. He currently is Vivian Gill Distinguished Research Professor at the George Washington University Medical Center, where he has also been Director of the Center for Family Research. His most notable contribution to the field came in 1981, when he published his monumental book, The Family's Construction of Reality.
Volition	Volition is the cognitive process by which an individual decides on and commits to a particular course of action. It is defined as purposive striving, and is one of the primary human psychological functions (the others being affection [affect or feeling], motivation [goals and expectations] and cognition [thinking]). Volitional processes can be applied consciously, and they can be automatized as habits over time.

Chapter 6. Change and Resistance

Therapy	Therapy is the attempted remediation of a health problem, usually following a diagnosis. In the medical field, it is synonymous with the word "treatment". Among psychologists, the term may refer specifically to psychotherapy or "talk therapy".
Therapeutic alliance	The therapeutic alliance refers to the relationship between a healthcare professional and a client (or patient). It is the means by which the professional hopes to engage with, and affect change in a client.
	While much early work on this subject was generated from a psychodynamic perspective, researchers from other orientations have since investigated this area. It has been found to predict treatment adherence (compliance) and concordance and outcome across a range of client/patient diagnoses and treatment settings. Research on the statistical power of the therapeutic relationship now reflects more than 1,000 findings.
Resistance	"Resistance" as initially used by Sigmund Freud, referred to patients blocking memories from conscious memory. This was a key concept, since the primary treatment method of Freud's talk therapy required making these memories available to the patient's consciousness.
	"Resistance" expanded
	Later, Freud described five different forms of resistance.
Credibility	Credibility refers to the objective and subjective components of the believability of a source or message.
	Traditionally, credibility has two key components: trustworthiness and expertise, which both have objective and subjective components. Trustworthiness is based more on subjective factors, but can include objective measurements such as established reliability.

Chapter 7. Change Techniques

Causality	Causality is the relationship between an event (the cause) and a second event (the effect), where the second event is understood as a consequence of the first.
	Though the causes and effects are typically related to changes or events, candidates include objects, processes, properties, variables, facts, and states of affairs; characterizing the causal relationship can be the subject of much debate.
	The philosophical treatment of causality extends over millennia.
Death	Death is the termination of the biological functions that sustain a living organism. The word refers both to the particular processes of life's cessation as well as to the condition or state of a formerly living body. Phenomena which commonly bring about death include predation, malnutrition, accidents resulting in terminal injury, and disease.
Salvador Minuchin	Salvador Minuchin is a family therapist born and raised in San Salvador, Entre Ríos, Argentina. He developed Structural Family Therapy, which addresses problems within a family by charting the relationships between family members, or between subsets of family. These charts represent power dynamics as well as the boundaries between different subsystems.
Nelson	Nelson is a piece of cricket slang terminology and superstition.
	The name, applied to team or individual scores of 111 or multiples thereof (known as double nelson, triple nelson, etc). is thought to refer to Lord Nelson's lost eye, arm and leg (Nelson actually had both of his legs intact, the third missing body part is mythical).
Intervention	An intervention is an orchestrated attempt by one, or often many, people (usually family and friends) to get someone to seek professional help with an addiction or some kind of traumatic event or crisis, or other serious problem. The term intervention is most often used when the traumatic event involves addiction to drugs or other items. Intervention can also refer to the act of using a technique within a therapy session.

Chapter 7. Change Techniques

Narrative	A narrative is a story that is created in a constructive format (as a work of speech, writing, song, film, television, video games, in photography or theatre) that describes a sequence of fictional or non-fictional events. Ultimately its origin is found in the Proto-Indo-European root gno-, "to know".
	The word "story" may be used as a synonym of "narrative", but can also be used to refer to the sequence of events described in a narrative.
Narrative therapy	Narrative Therapy is a form of psychotherapy using narrative. It was initially developed during the 1970s and 1980s, largely by Australian Michael White and his friend and colleague, David Epston, of New Zealand.
	Their approach became prevalent in North America with the 1990 publication of their book, Narrative Means to Therapeutic Ends, followed by numerous books and articles about previously unmanageable cases of anorexia nervosa, ADHD, schizophrenia, and many other problems.
Psychoeducation	Psychoeducation refers to the education offered to people who live with a psychological disturbance. Frequently psychoeducational training involves patients with schizophrenia, clinical depression, anxiety disorders, psychotic illnesses, eating disorders, and personality disorders, as well as patient training courses in the context of the treatment of physical illnesses. Family members are also included.
Communication	Communication is a process whereby meaning is defined and shared between living organisms. Communication requires a sender, a message, and an intended recipient, although the receiver need not be present or aware of the sender's intent to communicate at the time of communication; thus communication can occur across vast distances in time and space. Communication requires that the communicating parties share an area of communicative commonality.
Genogram	A genogram is a pictorial display of a person's family relationships and medical history. It goes beyond a traditional family tree by allowing the user to visualize hereditary patterns and psychological factors that punctuate relationships. It can be used to identify repetitive patterns of behavior and to recognize hereditary tendencies.

Chapter 7. Change Techniques

Coping	The psychological definition of coping is the process of managing taxing circumstances, expending effort to solve personal and interpersonal problems, and seeking "to master, minimize, reduce or tolerate stress" or conflict. Coping strategies In coping with stress, people tend to use one of the three main coping strategies: either appraisal-focused, problem-focused, or emotion-focused coping. Appraisal-focused strategies occur when the person modifies the way they think, for example: employing denial, or distancing oneself from the problem.
Family	In human context, a family is a group of people affiliated by consanguinity, affinity, or co-residence. In most societies it is the principal institution for the socialization of children. Extended from the human "family unit" by affinity, economy, culture, tradition, honor, and friendship are concepts of family that are metaphorical, or that grow increasingly inclusive extending to nationhood and humanism.
Triangulation	Triangulation is most commonly used to express a situation in which one family member will not communicate directly with another family member, but will communicate with a third family member, which can lead to the third family member becoming part of the triangle. The concept originated in the study of dysfunctional family systems, but can describe behaviors in other systems as well, including work. Triangulation can also be used as a label for a form of "splitting" in which one person plays the third family member against one that he or she is upset about.

Chapter 7. Change Techniques

Exploring	Exploring is a worksite-based program of Learning for Life, a subsidiary of the Boy Scouts of America, for young men and women who are 14 through 20 years old (15 through 21 in some areas). Exploring units, called "posts", usually have a focus on a single career field, such as police, fire/rescue, health, law, aviation, engineering, or the like, and may be sponsored by a government or business entity. Prior to the late 1990s, the Exploring program was the main BSA program for older youth and included posts with an emphasis on outdoor activities, which are now part of the Venturing program.
Household	The household is "the basic residential unit in which economic production, consumption, inheritance, child rearing, and shelter are organized and carried out"; [the household] "may or may not be synonymous with family". The household is the basic unit of analysis in many social, microeconomic and government models. The term refers to all individuals who live in the same dwelling.
Extended family	The term extended family has several distinct meanings. First, it is used synonymously with consanguineous family or joint family. Second, in societies dominated by the conjugal family or nuclear family, it is used to refer to kindred who does not belong to the conjugal family.
Reframing	The term reframing designates a communication technique which has origins in family systems therapy and the work of Virginia Satir. Milton H. Erickson has been associated with reframing and it also forms an important part of Neuro-linguistic programming. In addition, provocative therapy uses reframing with an emphasis on humor.
Play	Play refers to a range of voluntary, intrinsically motivated activities that are normally associated with pleasure and enjoyment. Play is essentially an activity which a person enjoys alone, though it can involve others, who perceive the play from their perspective and may not be in the mood for play. Play is most commonly associated with child activities, and when engaged in by an adult they may be described as "childish" or "child at heart".

Chapter 7. Change Techniques

Family Therapy	Family therapy, also referred to as couple and family therapy and family systems therapy, is a branch of psychotherapy that works with families and couples in intimate relationships to nurture change and development. It tends to view change in terms of the systems of interaction between family members. It emphasizes family relationships as an important factor in psychological health.

Chapter 8. Termination

Therapy	Therapy is the attempted remediation of a health problem, usually following a diagnosis. In the medical field, it is synonymous with the word "treatment". Among psychologists, the term may refer specifically to psychotherapy or "talk therapy".
Dropout	Dropout within the realm of electronics and electrical engineering, has a number of uses. It is the dropping away of a flake of magnetic material from magnetic tape, leading to loss of signal, or a failure to properly read a binary character from data storage. In magnetic disk, tape, card, or drum systems, a dropout is a recorded signal with an amplitude less than a predetermined percentage of a reference signal.
Therapeutic alliance	The therapeutic alliance refers to the relationship between a healthcare professional and a client (or patient). It is the means by which the professional hopes to engage with, and affect change in a client. While much early work on this subject was generated from a psychodynamic perspective, researchers from other orientations have since investigated this area. It has been found to predict treatment adherence (compliance) and concordance and outcome across a range of client/patient diagnoses and treatment settings. Research on the statistical power of the therapeutic relationship now reflects more than 1,000 findings.

Lightning Source UK Ltd.
Milton Keynes UK
UKHW051924011219
354478UK00018B/155/P